Maria Luisa Polid

CIVITA
and
BAGNOREGIO

BONECHI EDIZIONI "IL TURISMO" FIRENZE

Agent and Distributor for Latium (excluding Rome):
Archidee (Claudio Tini)
Località Sant'Egidio
01032 Caprarola (VT)
Tel. and Fax 0761 647540

"I would never have become a writer unless I had lived
for a few months every year, from July to November,
starting in my earliest youth, in the valley of Civita,
with the vision of the white crests, the golden volcanic clay,
the eloquent ruins, in the land of Saint Bonaventure,
the city that is dying..."

BONAVENTURA TECCHI

Managing Editor: Barbara Bonechi

Photographic references: Publisher's archives
Photo R. Gambacorta – Studio G.S.G. (Bagnoregio – VT)
Photo P.P. Giacobbi - Studio G.S.G. (Bagnoregio – VT)
Photo Claudio Tini (Caprarola – VT)
Aerial view on page 4 taken by: Foto Palozzi, conc. S.M.A., nr. 119 on 18.2.94.

Reproduction of the following illustrations by kind concession of the "Progetto Civita" Association: page 4 (from C. Margottini, "Evoluzione morfologica dell'area di Civita di Bagnoregio in tempi storici"); page 5, bottom (from the research material collected by ENEA for the Progetto Civita:"Osservazioni geologiche e monitoraggio storico dell'ambiente"); page 19, the material is published in the volume entitled "Civita di Bagnoregio: l'ambiente, la memoria, il progetto", edited by the Progetto Civita Association, Rome, 1990.

Layout: Sabrina Menicacci

Iconographical research: Lorena Lazzari

English translation: Anna Moore Valeri

Photolithographs: Fotolito Immagine, Florence

Publisher: La Zincografica Fiorentina, Florence

ISBN 88-7204-424-3

The publishers wishes to state that every effort has been made to identify and to locate all those persons who may have legitimate copyright claims on the photographic and illustrative material used in this guide. Should any omissions have been made in this sense, anyone who considers himself legally entitled to payment for reasons of copyright may contact the publisher at the address indicated above.

"THE DYING CITY"

If you observe it from a distance as it clings to the edge of the precipice which seems to be attacking it from all sides, the village of Civita di Bagnoregio seems like a ghost town, something that could exist only in the mind of a visionary or in a dream remembered.

Especially on certain misty mornings that little group of houses seems to float surrounded by a fog of unreality. Civita, like an island in our memory or a figment of our imagination, is connected by a single narrow cement walkway to reality and to the surrounding countryside; it is inaccessible to modern means of transportation and takes us far away, not so much in distance as in time.

In fact, as one gradually starts to cross this walkway suspended in the air – only 900 feet, but it seems endless – there is a feeling that one is leaving the real world, and this feeling becomes even stronger after entering the ancient city gate of Santa Maria, standing guard over a sheer drop between the remains of two houses with their windows opened wide over the emptiness.

One almost has the impression that this gate opens into a supernatural world, surviving in another dimension. And yet, there are plants on the terraces, flowers on the window sills, people moving in the streets, wives and peasants returning

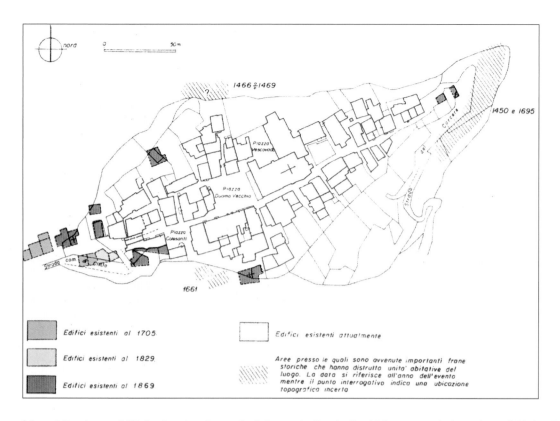

Map of the town of Civita showing its gradual decay starting in the 15th century; *below:* **view of Civita di Bagnoregio.**

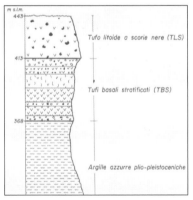

Below: **Geological formation of the cliffs of Civita; stratigraphic survey made by the ENEA institute for the Civita Project;** *above:* **The valley of the calanchi (eroded clay hills).**

from the fields with their donkeys, but it is all in a strangely hushed atmosphere without the noise and stress to which our cities have inured us, in other words it is just as people lived hundreds of years ago. The sensation of emptiness, the void can almost be touched: a street which drops off into the precipice, the façade of a house with nothing behind it.

The miracle of Civita is this: a remnant of the past miraculously surviving the passage of time and natural adversities which have changed a rich and prosperous city into a dying town, destined to perish but still clinging to life. This refusal to die is evident in the stubborn persistence of the people who still remain (only about twenty people live in the town all year round; in the Summer the population is about 300), in the meticulous care with which the streets and houses are maintained, and in the enthusiasm for the initiatives which have sprung up for the purpose of giving it new hope to continue to exist.

The most recent of these is the "Civita Project" initiated in 1988 by an association formed of public and private institutions with the intention of creating a research center for the study of new technologies for the conservation and the appreciation of our environmental and cultural heritage.

For this reason Civita has become a symbol of the precarious condition in which a great part of Italy's monuments are now to be found, and hopefully, will also become a kind of 'mascot' representing the determination to conserve and renew in order to give a future to our past.

Before reaching Civita, the best view of the village is from the terraces of the nearby town of Lubriano, next to the lovely little 18th century church of the Madonna del Poggio, or from the terrace of Bagnoregio. This village, once just a little suburb of the older and more important city of Civita, is now a lively center for agriculture, commerce and light industry with a population of about 4000; all of the public buildings which once stood on terrain which has been swallowed up in the landslides at Civita were gradually moved here.

From these two observation points it is easier to understand the nature of the terrain where Civita was built and the origin of the landslides which, after having caused a major upheaval in the geological layers in the zone, are now laying siege to the last little outpost of houses hovering together in the center of what looks like a lunar landscape or a crater formed by the fall of a gigantic meteorite.

Civita di Bagnoregio is perched on top of a hill at an altitude of 1440 ft. above sea level, between two valleys running in an East-West direction and in which two streams flow: the Rio Chiaro to the North-East and the Rio Torbido to the South.

The hill is made up of a layer of tufa (a soft volcanic stone typical of central Italy) about 200 ft. thick which was formed after a series of volcanic eruptions between 700,000 and 125,000 years ago. This layer of solidified lava lies on an unstable base of clay and sand.

The numerous shell fossils which have been found in the terrain have made it possible to date the formation to about a million years ago, i.e., to the Lower Pleistocene era. This was a period of major geological upheaval in which volcanoes sank and lakes arose from the bottom of the sea in the area between the river Tiber and the Tyrrhenian Sea.

The clay on the bottom of the valleys is continually eroded by the two impetuous streams and washed away by the torrential rains, leaving bare portions of the tufa bank above, which, without a solid base, soon break off and crumble to the bottom of the valley, leaving new banks of clay exposed along the slopes, and so the whole process of erosion starts over again.

The Italian-Argentine poet Juan Rodolfo Wilcock (1919-1978) was particularly attached to this area and became a resident of Lubriano from where he could observe this desolate landscape, which he described with a mixture of scientific precision and lyrical vision in this poem:

The valley of the calanchi in which the eerie landscape appears like a crater on the moon.

"A layer of whitish chalk,
a strip of sandy clay,
a layer of volcanic powder,
a deposit of marine detritus,
a vein of spongy lime,
a mantle of lava pressing down
on the sand,
entire eras weighing upon
the last traces of life
on this planet."

The terrain where Civita stands is therefore particularly unstable and this problem must have become apparent even to the earliest inhabitants of the area, who must have been Etruscans, as the many archeological finds would tend to indicate, or perhaps even Villanovan (9th-8th century BC) according to some scholars on the basis of a few artifacts which, however, were both fragmentary and without archeological context.

The Etruscans had tried to harness the rainwater and control the flow of the streams by building a system of canals, traces of which are still visible on the cliff where Civita was built. But in the general confusion which prevailed as the Roman Empire slowly collapsed, the maintenance of the drainage tanks was neglected and the clay became impregnated with water. At the same time, the intense exploitation of the area for agricultural purposes caused the gradual reduction of the number of trees which had always helped to hold the terrain firm with their roots. The erosion of the terrain began in this way and soon reached the city; entire neighborhoods were swallowed up as they dropped off in the landslides, until only the central and most ancient part of the village was left.

While probably repeating parts of early documents which have not come down to us, the first edition of the Statutes of the Commune in 1373 already contained a series of precautions which were to be taken to protect the environment: "Nobody may dig caves in the cliffs around the village of Civita; transgressors will be fined 100 *soldi* for each offense; nor may anyone dig beneath the city streets.....nobody may excavate beneath the locality of the Friars or take their animals to graze beneath the cliffs".

In 1450 the convent of the nuns of St. Clare in the zone called "Carcere" south-east of the village began to give way, a

The valley of the calanchi and the cliffs of Civita as seen from the terrace of Lubriano.

**A panoramic view
of the valley of the calanchi.**

group of houses towards Lubriano collapsed between 1446 and 1469, and in 1553 the street that led to the Porta di Ponte began to fall in. From then on the chronicles of the city mention with increasing frequency landslides, floods, collapses, mudslides, and the formation of cracks and chasms, which year after year gradually eat up the village. The situation became even more serious as a result of the disastrous earthquakes of 1695 and 1764. But in the past, starting in 280 BC up until 1349 AD the area had frequently been involved in seismic activity, just as it has been in recent times. The village is located in a seismic zone which is formed around a series of volcanic lakes which include the dry lake in the crater of Amiata, the lake of Bolsena and to the South, the lakes of Vico and Bracciano, and others down below Rome.

Unfortunately, besides the damage caused by natural disasters, there have also been man-made ones: in 1944 German troops blew up the masonry bridge which was the last remaining connection between Civita and the rest of the town. Landslides occurred in 1964 causing the newly rebuilt bridge to collapse shortly before its inauguration.

In the *Liber Consiliorum*, the book where the decisions of the town council were registered, alternating with the notations concerning the landslides, collapses and demolitions, we find an almost endless list of measures taken by the authorities to try to remedy the disasters and prevent new ones. There were severe laws which prohibited the cutting of trees, or allowing animals to graze at the base of the cliff, which ordered the planting of trees along the banks of the two streams, the Chiaro and the Torbido, the filling in of the caves which had been dug in the cliffs (many of which were

**Another view
of the valley of the calanchi.**

One of the most unusual 'calanchi' formations, this one is called "the Cathedral".

ancient Etruscan chamber tombs being reused as dove-cotes, stalls and tool sheds). It was also forbidden to remove clay for making pots along the road which went from Civita to Mercatello and Rota. Below are some examples of city ordinances:

1564 – "It is forbidden to extract sand, to deviate the waters, to fail to fill in cracks or to fill in the cotes with bricks…"

1583 – " the bridge of Varco is falling into ruin and must be repaired…"

1603 – "There is danger of falling and breaking ones neck when walking along the road which goes from San Francesco to Mercatello; surveyors must be sent to inspect it…"

1608 – "The gateway to Civita is about to collapse and this could occur in 8-10 days; measures to prevent this must be taken immediately, and it may be necessary to make a new road or a new gateway…"

1730 – "In consideration of the damage caused by the animals, especially the goats, grazing is forbidden…"

1758 – "Since the road to Civita is ruined it must be repaired; an architect must be called in…"

1765 – "Trees must be planted; laborers must be hired to plant them…"

1786 – "Nobody may dare, under any pretext or for any reason, to cut or order another to cut wood, trees or branches of any kind; this is ordered for the purpose of conserving the road.

Finally, in 1819, since all attempts to shore up the terrain had turned out to be useless, Civita was evacuated and the inhabitants were moved to the nearby hamlet of Bagnoregio which was built on more stable terrain and where the Bishopric had already been moved in 1699 to the new Church of Saint Nicholas.

Many inhabitants refused to go and decided "to stay where they were in consideration of the convenience for their work" and another century went by before the conditions in Civita became so serious that even the last inhabitants decided to move elsewhere, leaving forever the village to which they were so attached.

Attempts to consolidate the terrain continued: new trees were planted, fences and retaining walls were built, and recently, from 1959 to 1961, a new experimental technique was tested: the electro-geo-chemical consolidation of the terrain made by applying electrical current to the clay layers in order to transform their physio-chemical structure.

"The graceful doorways of compact eternal stone" (B. Tecchi).

Each time however, landslides, floods and earthquakes have made vain all of man's efforts; yet Civita continues to resist, clinging to the top of its tiny pinnacle.

As part of the "Civita Project" there are major environmental engineering projects now being studied with the hope of finding a way of saving what remains of the town without altering the appearance of the surrounding area. Perhaps it will be electronics and computers that save the "dying city", surrounded by the hills of eroded clay called *calanchi* which continually change shape as they are altered by wind and rain. Once houses stood here, the fields bloomed, cattle grazed, and the forests were verdant; now all of this is covered with sand.

Bonaventura Tecchi dedicated this famous passage to Civita, in which he expresses the affection he felt for his hometown:

The only road, narrow and white like a ribbon, which leads from the little black huddle of houses, an island rising high in the midst of a sea of chalk and chasms, to the world beyond, to the terrain that is stable and safe, is about to collapse. It already fell in once a few years ago and miraculously just a tiny strip of rock remained standing; engi-

One of the typical narrow streets of Civita.

neers and brick-layers came running. They built slender arches over the void and drove pillars and foundations into the ground. But the silent persistence of the streams at the bottom of the valleys, the deep and secret sliding away of the clay, the never ending rains have again eaten away in just a few years a structure which was supposed to be solid and long-lasting. In a few months, or perhaps within a few days, maybe during one of those rainy winter nights, this bridge, the only tenuous connection, will fall...

I went again to get a good look, before it's too late. I saw Civita as it must have appeared in antiquity to our distant ancestors, closed up like a black fist high on its rocky perch, like some kind of medieval war machine or solid fortress. I remembered that over the medieval arch at the gateway to the city there are still two snarling rampant lions, one of which seems to be grappling with something that the atmos-

Next page: **the cliffs of Civita seen from below. Deep cracks are visible in the rocky layers underneath the houses perched on the edge of the abyss.**

pheric agents and the hand of man have destroyed; the images that came to my mind on this occasion were certainly not idyllic or peaceful.

The walls of the few houses which were still left standing seemed to be terribly dark that day, and rough and wrinkled; but the graceful doorways, of compact, eternal stone, the decorations that artists had chiseled on them, the heraldic emblems over the windows, more than ever spoke to me of long-gone gentility...

The ancient village is condemned; a few years more, but its fate is now certain. It is surrounded on all sides by air, and is more of a miracle than an actual thing, more legend than reality. Its name is ancient and simple: Civita, without adjectives or specifications. Its place, far from the major highways is in the heart of Italy; but it could be the name of many other Italian villages suspended halfway between the rude and the polite, solidly realistic amidst the crude volcanic bareness of the tufa rock and the chalk hills and at the same time dream-like and apocalyptic. I suddenly felt that this attachment to the land, to the houses, to the ruined walls was a thing that was exclusively ours, Italian, especially for certain central Italian villages, perched up on their high rocky hills, refusing to die because they had already seen centuries of deaths and rebirths." (Bonaventura Tecchi *"Antica Terra"*).

View of the inhabited part of Civita in which one can note the profferlo, the external stairway with balcony typical of Viterbo and surrounding areas.

The history of Civita and Bagnoregio

The first artifacts found in the territory of Bagnoregio date to the Stone Age: axes, arrow heads, knives belonging to the Neolithic. There are no remains from the Bronze Age, probably due to the fact that in the middle of the second millenium BC there was an increase in volcanic activity in the area around the Volsini mountains, near what is now the lake of Bolsena. In fact this lake is the result of a series of earthquakes and volcanic eruptions which culminated with the sinking of the crater and the formation of the lake in the middle.

As has been mentioned, the first noteworthy traces of human occupation belong to the Etruscan era and include numerous chamber tombs excavated around the ancient city, which incidentally, had a typically Etruscan urban layout. It was built on a narrow plateau which had an East-West orientation that overlooked the plain below and was bordered on two sides by the streams we have already spoken of. This position assured strong natural defenses and the availability of drinking water, the two most important factors required for guaranteeing the safety of the city and its ability to resist in case of a prolonged siege. These characteristics are typical of Etruscan cities; another typical feature of Etruscan settlements was the custom of digging

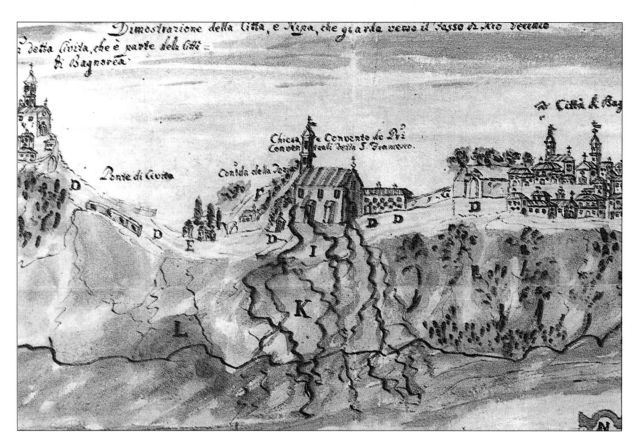

The area around Civita and Bagnoregio as it appeared in 1765; in the center is the Convent of San Francesco and other buildings which no longer exist. This drawing was enclosed with the report of F. Antolini which was sent by the Municipality of Bagnoregio to the Sacro Congregazione del Buon Governo in Rome.

caves around the inhabited area for the burial of the deceased, so that the city of the living and the city of the dead were separate and distinct but near to each other and visible as a constant reminder.

Unfortunately, many of the tombs have been destroyed by the landslides which have eroded the cliff and the surrounding plain, but the descriptions left us by historians and archeologists who had seen them, the quality of the artifacts found inside and the appearance of those that still remain, like the so-called Cave of St. Bonaventure, have made it possible to determine that an Etruscan city of a certain importance was located here in the 8th century BC. To the East stood an Acropolis, the highest and most strategically important point in the area, where the religious and civic buildings of the community were situated. The heart of the Etruscan city was where the village of Civita now stands, and the meaning of the word *civita* reminds us that this was the "city" par excellence. It now occupies only a part of the Etruscan Acropolis, as more than a third of it has been devoured by earthquakes. The city owed its importance to the fact that it was located along an ancient and heavily trafficked road which led from the Valley of the Tiber River to the Lake of Bolsena, and crossed several important roads which lead from the ports of the Tyrrhenian Sea inland to the Apennine Mountains, forming a dense network of trade routes.

Flowers and plants
soften the appearance
of the stone walls.

Preceding page: **The steep
walkway which replaced
the old path down the slope
to the ford in the Tiber river.**

To the East the expansion of the city was limited by natural barriers; for this reason the city spread westward toward what was called the neighborhood of Rota, which is now Bagnoregio. The two cities are now separated by a chasm and connected only by a narrow footbridge. They were once a single city, joined with other neighborhoods like Ponte to the West and Carcere to the East, but these latter, swallowed up by the landslides, have totally disappeared. The place name, Bagnoregio, is of Early Medieval origin and is derived from *Balneum regis*, the bath of the king, in connection with the hot springs which existed in the area and whose salutary waters cured the wounds and healed the sores of a king who bathed there. The numerous sulphurous and ferruginous hot springs which still exist in the area, like that of Acquarossa and Bulicame near Viterbo, confirm that this custom was still widely in use in the 16th century. In the Statutes of Bagnoregio dated 1373, a hot spring near the town is mentioned and this is not surprising in consideration of the continual volcanic activity in the zone. According to some scholars the king the springs were named for was the Lombard Desiderius, according to others the name started to be used at the beginning of the 6th century AD.

The name Bagnoregio was altered over the years until it became Bagnorea but was restored to the original spelling by a Royal Decree of April 18th 1922 and at this time Civita became a *frazione* or suburb of the Municipality. Originally it was Bagnoregio that was a suburb of the more important city, Civita, the urban layout of which, as we have seen, was typically Etruscan, with the main streets meeting at right-angles: the *decumanus* ran from East to West, and still today divides the town in two, and the *cardo* ran along the North-South axis. The point where the streets met was the forum, the main plaza of the town. In the walls of the bell-tower and other buildings there are archeological remains of the Roman era which confirm the continuous occupation of the urban settlement. The Romans subjugated the nearby Etruscan city of Volsini in 265 BC and that date marks the end of the Etruscan domination of this city. During the Christian era, according to the ancient chronicles, the martyr Saint Ansano was born here and worked miracles and conversions before being imprisoned in Civita and then put to death in Siena in 303 AD.

The presence of a diocese is recorded in Bagnoregio around the year 600; this is one of the oldest dioceses in the area and confirms the importance of the town in the Early Middle Ages. During this period the town was almost continually subjected to siege; it was first occupied by the Goths (493-553), then by the Byzantines (553-605), and then was dominated by the Lombards. After the pact of Quiersy (754) Pipino, king of the Franks, had promised the Pope that he would return all of the territories which had been occupied by the Lombards as soon as he had defeated them. Charlemagne kept this promise and in 774 Bagnoregio became part of the Papal State.

Afterwards the city was dominated by a long series of feudal lords, including the Monaldeschi who became lords of Orvieto. In 1140 the city finally obtained status as a free Commune and a period of prosperity and intense cultural and artistic activity followed.

After Saint Ansano, the city, which had been the birthplace of two other saints (Bernardo Janni in the 8th century and Hildebrand who died in 873), in the 13th century gained further stature as the birthplace of one of the most important figures of Christianity: Saint Bonaventure (1217-1274), general of the Franciscan order, cardinal and professor of theology at the University of Paris.

The house where he was born in Civita, which was transformed into a religious building, is long since gone, swallowed up like so many others by the landslides and earthquakes. The convent of St. Francis, halfway between the neighborhoods of Civita and Rota, where Bonaventure lived after taking his vows, has also disappeared.

Saint Bonaventure's real name was Giovanni Fidanza and he was the son of a wealthy doctor and his wife, who was particularly devoted to St. Francis. The little friar from Assisi had come to the city to preach in the years between 1219 and 1222, and had founded a community there. The little boy Giovanni had fallen seriously ill and seemed about to die when he was miraculously cured by the prayers of his mother who had implored St. Francis to intercede. From that moment on, the name of the boy became Bonaventure (good fortune) and his fate was inextricably bound to that of the Saint from Assisi. Francis had given him life again, and

Following pages: **Views of the town of Civita.**

Bonaventure consecrated this life to the Saint and took the vows of the Franciscan order shortly after he turned 23. After having completed his studies at Bagnoregio he went to study at the University of the Sorbonne in Paris. One of his classmates in the theological program was St. Thomas Aquinas, and the two became close friends.

Bonaventure was first nominated professor of theology and later in 1257 he was chosen as General Minister of the Order, which was going through a period of grave moral and organizational crisis which Bonaventure was able to resolve with great ability, to the extent that he was often called "the second founder of the Franciscan order". On the other hand

Bonaventure's talent for negotiation was often used in order to resolve difficult situations, like the time he was sent by the Pope to England to try to find a diplomatic solution to the disagreement between the Papacy and the English Court, or his mediation during the hotly disputed Conclave of Viterbo which lasted for three years, from 1268 to 1271.

It was on this famous occasion that the exasperated populace of Viterbo decided to segregate the cardinals in the palace and removed part of the roof in order to leave them exposed to the inclement weather. They had taken very seriously a statement that Bonaventure had made jokingly – but not totally – that "the Palace should be uncovered in order to let the Holy Spirit come in and illuminate the Sacred College". (According to another version of the story this statement was made by the English cardinal of York). In any case thanks to the mediation of Bonaventure, the Conclave was finally able to elect Gregory X. This pope soon became aware of the grave situation in which the Church had come to find itself and appointed Bonaventure to organize an Ecumenical Council which was held in the city of Lyons. The purpose of the Council was to enact important and urgent reforms in the Church of Rome, which was afflicted by corruption and torn apart by rivalries, and to attempt a reunification with the Greek Church. The pope also wished to organize a Crusade to free the Holy Land from the Saracens. This was a grave responsibility for Bonaventure and was probably the cause of his death, which occurred in July of 1274 soon after the Council was opened. According to one tradition, he was poisoned because the reforms he was trying to promote were to advanced to meet with the approval of the ecclesiastical hierarchy.

A remarkable figure both as a mystic and theologian, Bonaventure was greatly admired for his profound culture, his moral prestige and his talents as an organizer, but was a man of great humility.

It is said that when the messengers sent by the Pope arrived to announce that he had been appointed cardinal and to give him the insignia of his new office, Bonaventure asked them to wait until he had finished washing the dishes of the frairs because it was his turn to clean up the kitchen in the monastery, and, not knowing where to put the purple mantle and the cardinal's hat, he hung them on a tree!

Another noteworthy figure in art history who was a native of Bagnoregio was Francesco Monaldeschi, who as Bishop of Orvieto promoted the construction of the Cathedral and lay the first stone of the building in 1290; five years later when he was transferred to Florence, he also placed the first stone which marked the start of construction on the great Cathedral of Santa Maria del Fiore.

During the Middle Ages, life in Bagnoregio was not much

different from that in other small Communes in the area, constantly involved in wars and sieges; it was able to maintain a relative amount of autonomy in consideration of the fact that it belonged to the Papal State and was under constant threat on the part of its neighbor and rival, Orvieto. In 1457 the people of Bagnoregio destroyed the mighty Fortress of the Cervara in order to avert the danger of a return of the tyrannical Monaldeschi family, and in 1494 they refused to receive King Charles VIII of France who had asked them for hospitality as he marched south to Rome and Naples.

This act of courage however was not awarded with the gratitude that might have been expected on the part of the Pope, Alexander VI Borgia, who just two years later returned the favor by creating a regime of cardinal-governors appointed by the Pope, which of course placed severe limitations on the liberty of the Commune.

The first of this long series of governors was a compatriot of the Pope, Ferdinand of Castile, who had the cathedral restored and the Bishopric enlarged and decorated. The position was considered one of great prestige and was usually conferred on illustrious ecclesiastical personages. The most famous cardinal-governor was the English cardinal Reginald Pole, Duke of Suffolk, who had been persecuted and finally exiled by Henry VIII for his Catholic faith (1547).

The regime of the cardinal-governors lasted until 1612 when the city came to depend on the apostolic legation of Viterbo

The Stanza della Segnatura in the Vatican, painting of the Disputation of the Sacrament by Raphael. St. Bonaventure is shown dressed in his Cardinal's costume, in prayer in front of the Doctors of the Church (the seventh person from the center, lower right).

which was governed by a layman and a group of priests who had sworn that the ancient communal statutes would be respected.

In this era life in the city was relatively quiet. It was a prosperous agricultural center which exported large quantities of typical local wines like Moscatello and Lambrusco, olive oil, vegetables and quality fruit like the "pink apple". The Papal Court particularly appreciated these products, above all a special variety of celery, cheese and sausage meats.

The nearby oak woods of Farnia furnished lumber for the ships of the Papal fleet. Basalt was mined in a quarry in the area and was used for making millstones. Another important product, vitriol, was extracted from nearby mines. Besides these sources of income, there was also a prosperous textile industry, especially for the production of wool.

There were no particular economic or political problems, as is evident from this passage written by a historian in 1622:

"These people are inclined to fun and pleasant conversation, but they are also used to war and to liberty, and are fiercely adverse to servitude and being subjugated. And it is in the first of these things however that they have wonderfully succeeded, in the competitions, the plays and the

contests and races, the masked balls and the dancing, especially in these last two they have always excelled and still excel today. For at Mardi Gras time they dance in the two plazas of Civita and of Rota publicly and in a licentious way, and men and woman of every age and social condition participate, all masked in the strangest ways, but in particular the women, who dance all day to the sound of the fife..." (P. Romani "Pentalitologia", 1622).

This passage describes the last carefree years before a long series of tragic events which started with the earthquake of 1695, which began on June 2nd and continued with violent tremors almost every day until July 15th. Thirty-two people were killed and every building in Rota and Civita suffered at least partial damage. A new earthquake took place the following year, then again in 1702 and 1703, in 1707 the Torbido stream was blocked by a landslide causing the formation of stagnant pools which brought about a terrible epidemic of malaria. More earthquakes followed in 1717, 1738, 1743, 1755, 1759, 1764, 1783, 1785, 1789, 1873, 1881, 1903...

An endless series of landslides took place after each period of seismic activity; the neighborhood of Civita was especially hard hit and in 1699 the authorities decided to transfer the Cathedral and the Bishopric to Rota for greater safety. The road which joined the two neighborhoods collapsed and all the buildings which stood along it including the ancient Palazzo del Comune or city hall. By this time Civita was almost totally isolated. In 1901 a detour was made in the road so that it would pass on the south slope of the Valley of the Torbido where there was less risk of landslides.

The buildings, many of which were of exceptional artistic and historic value, and which have now disappeared into the desert of clay, are too numerous to list. The history of Bagnoregio is marked far more by these events than by political vicissitudes. After a brief period under the Roman Republic instituted by the French in 1798, followed by a brief time under Napoleonic domination from 1809 to 1814, the city again became part of the Papal States and remained so until 1870. During the Risorgimento (struggle for the unification of Italy) in 1849 the city adhered to the new Republic governed by Mazzini, Armellini and Saffi; in 1867 the first battle between the Papal Militia and Garibaldi's volunteers took place here and is known to history as the "Battle of Bagnorea".

The name Bagnoregio gradually began to replace that of Civita in the chronicles and histories, while the ancient village continued to cling to its increasingly precarious perch. The public buildings, the convents and the cathedral had already been transferred when, in 1922, the government finally ordered the evacuation of Civita and the removal of all

Preceding page: **The roofs of Civita.**

One of the most characteristic streets of Civita,
the Via de Macelli and the gate,
Porta Santa Maria.

its inhabitants to a safer place. At first the order was ignored and the people of Civita refused to leave their houses but the abandonment took place gradually, not because it was imposed by force of law but by force of nature, as landslides continued to eat away at the few remaining buildings. Finally in 1951, thanks to the involvement of the writer Bonaventura Tecchi who was born here, the problem of the "dying city" was brought to the attention of the authorities, scientists, and the cultural élite.

Two years later Tecchi created the Center of Bonaventure Studies which organizes annual meetings with studies dedicated to the Franciscan saint. Archeological excavations were conducted, restorations were made and consolidation work was carried out on the terrain. Fellini directed one of his most famous films "La Strada" in Bagnoregio, and the town was suddenly discovered by artists who came to enjoy its incomparable landscape.

For centuries Civita has continued to fight its battle against a fate that seems inevitable. All attempts at reconstruction and recovery have up to now given disappointing results. The "Civita Project" represents a source of renewed hope thanks mainly to the new possibilities offered by technological progress.

A VOYAGE IN THE PAST

Bagnoregio is located in the Province of Viterbo, almost at the border between the regions of Latium and Umbria. It is reached by taking the Via Cassia road to Montefiascone and then heading towards Orvieto until, after about 6 miles, you encounter the road to Bagnoregio on the right. You can also get there from Viterbo by following the provincial road which runs parallel to the Tiber (and for this reason is called La Teverina) or on the Autostrada del Sole, turning off at the exit for Orvieto.

Our visit begins at the gateway of this lively little city, whose animated atmosphere creates such a contrast with the isolation and the silence of Civita. The prevalently Renaissance

Bagnoregio - The Albana gate, made by Ippolito Scalza.

origins of the town are evident in the urban layout and the style of the buildings, which are more recent than those of the ancient civic center which one by one gave away its public buildings, its cathedral, its palazzi and houses which were destroyed and never rebuilt or moved away to more stable terrain.

At the entrance to the city there is a wide plaza shaded by linden trees. To the left we can observe a monument erected in honor of the volunteers of Garibaldi who died in the Battle of Bagnorea in October 1867. Nearby there is a Memorial Park where the veterans of the First World War planted pine trees and cedars of Lebanon in memory of their dead compatriots. Each tree has a name on it as a memorial.

Proceeding, we find an open area with the monumental "Porta Albana"

Bagnoregio - Inside of the Cathedral dedicated to Saints Nicholas, Bonaventure and Donatus.

which was built between 1586 and 1589 according to a design furnished by the famous Orvieto architect, Ippolito Scalza, and inspired by examples of Roman Triumphal Arches. It once stood in the midst of a crenellated portion of the city walls which had been rebuilt in 1906 and then torn down in 1922 to facilitate access to the city, as traffic began to increase.

On the right there is a little circular temple which recalls the one designed by Bramante. It is dedicated to St. Bonaventure and was designed by the Viterbese, Pietro Gagliardi in 1856. Inside is an altar painting which was made by Friar Silvestro of the Carmelite order for the sixth centenary of the death of St. Bonaventure in 1874.

Proceeding along Via Roma, the visitor can admire a series of noble buildings like the Palazzo Cibo-Gualterio (1559), Palazzo Nobili-Venturini (1600) and Palazzo Vittori-Antiseri (second half of the 16th century). We soon reach Piazza Cavour, in the center of which there is a Monument to the Dead of all the Wars designed by the Roman architect Oriolo Frezzotti in 1929, which was inspired by an ancient Roman altar, and reflects the artistic style of the era.

On the right we can observe the Cathedral with the Bishop's Palace to the side and a slender bell-tower. It was built where an ancient church dedicated to Santa Maria della Neve had once stood and was restored in 1606 to replace the decaying parish church of San Nicola.

When Civita was seriously damaged in the earthquake of 1695 and it was feared that even the Cathedral of San Donato might collapse, the Papal authorities decided to transfer the Episcopal title to this building, which from 1699 began to be remodeled, enlarged and embellished and this continued throughout the 18th and 18th centuries. It is now consecrated to Saints Nicholas, Donatus and Bonaventure.

One of the most interesting objects which is preserved in the last chapel on the right is the precious reliquary of the Santo Braccio (Holy Arm) which was made by a French goldsmith in 1490 using gold and silver which had been donated by the people of the city. They had requested, in fact, a reliquary for "their" saint to be kept in his native city. As mentioned earlier, St. Bonaventure had died in France and was buried in Lyons in a church that was soon abandoned

Cathedral of Bagnoregio.
From left to right: **a precious reliquary containing the bible which belonged to St. Bonaventure; the Reliquary del Santo Braccio (of the Holy Arm), by a French goldsmith of the end of the 15th century, made of gold and silver donated by the people of Civita; it contains the right arm of St. Bonaventure.**

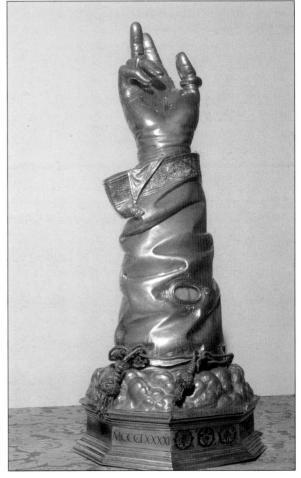

because it was collapsing. In 1450 his remains were moved to a more decorous location and in 1492 Bonaventure was canonized. The king of France, Charles VIII, who was particularly devoted to the Saint, in order to favor the outcome of his expedition to Italy in 1490 had had his remains exhumed, adorned with precious vestments, and ceremoniously reburied. It was on this occasion that the General of the Franciscan order, Francesco Sansone, requested for the citizens, and was granted, the right arm of the Saint, and it was brought to Bagnoregio in a famous procession in 1491. It is the only relic that remains, as all of the others were burnt by the Huguenots in 1562 or lost during the French Revolution. Another interesting object that is kept here is a parchment Bible decorated with beautiful illuminations; according to tradition, it once belonged to St. Bonaventure, who made notes in the margins.

In the center of the choir is a Roman sarcophagus of the 1st century AD which was used in the church as a Communion altar and on which a pagan myth is depicted, Diana and her youthful lover, Endymion. On the chariot of the moon, drawn by two horses across the celestial vault, the goddess stops to contemplate the handsome young shepherd who lies in a deep sleep. The sarcophagus had been used for the removal of the remains of the Bishop, St. Hildebrand from the Cathedral of San Donato, and after various vicissitudes was rediscovered in a garden.

Cathedral of Bagnoregio. St. Mary Magdalene by the Viterbese painter Pietro Vanni (1845-1905).

Also worthy of note, is the painting of St. Mary Magdalene by Pietro Vanni, a 19th century painter from Viterbo. It is located in the last chapel of the left nave.

As we leave the Cathedral and continue our walk along Via Mazzini we soon reach a tree shaded plaza: on the right there is the city hall (Palazzo Comunale) which has recently been remodeled. It was originally in the neighborhood of Mercatello on the road that leads to Civita, but because of the precarious condition of the terrain it was first transferred to Civita in 1448 and then to Bagnoregio after the earthquake of 1695.

Farther on, to the left, is the monument to St. Bonaventure by Cesare Aureli (1897) and the Church of the Annunciation. It was restored in 1933 and the simple harmonious lines of the original Romanesque and Gothic style are now visible. The bell-tower was built in 1735. Inside there are remains of several fine frescoes: a *Madonna and Child with Saints Bartholomew and James* by the Viterbese artist, Giovan Francesco di Avanzarano (1504); on the right, Saint Victoria martyr, one of the Patron Saints of the City.

To the left, a fine 15th century Crucifix and a fresco depicting Santa Monica opening her mantle held by two Angels, in order to protect her faithful from Divine Punishment. This painting with its rather naif style and charming details, like the frieze above it, is by Giovan Francesco di Avanzarano (1506).

The adjacent 13th century convent was rebuilt in 1528 by the architect Michele Sanmicheli. The cloister is well worth a visit; in the center is a well, designed by the Orvietan architect Ippolito Scalza in 1604.

Continuing on our walk, we reach the "Belvedere" or Terrace of old St. Francis where we can enjoy the splendid panorama of Civita and the valleys beyond it. The terrace is named for the monastery founded by St. Francis, according to tradition, and in which St. Bonaventure studied. Nothing of it remains, but it is said that St. Francis stopped here to pray in an ancient Etruscan tomb which is still known today as the "Cave of St. Francis" and this is where the miraculous healing of little Giovanni Fidanza took place. The cave is still visible at the end of the terrace.

The road once continued on in a straight line toward Civita and was a wide tree-lined avenue used by horses and carriages; it collapsed in a landslide in 1901.

If we now go back a few yards and turn left in Via Bonaventura Tecchi, we will soon reach the place where the Mercatello neighborhood was. There was a large plaza here where they held fairs and markets and the city hall and other important buildings were built here. It was a lively neighborhood and the center of commerce in the city. Now only a little group of houses is huddled here surrounded by a great void.

This is where the cement footbridge to Civita starts; it was built to replace the stone one built in

Corso Mazzini in Bagnoregio; to the right is the Palazzo dei Priori which was remodeled in 1523. After the disastrous earthquake of 1695 the municipal government was transferred here from Civita.

Church of the Annunciation:
St. Anthony (1408);
right: **Santa Monica Protecting her Faithful by the Viterbese painter Giovan Francesco d'Avanzarano.**

Preceding page: **Bagnoregio - Façade and interior of the Church of the Annunciation.**

1920 which the Nazis destroyed with explosives in 1944. For more than twenty years there was only a narrow wooden footbridge connecting Civita to the rest of the world; the present-day bridge in cement was built in 1965, and, as mentioned, part of it collapsed even before it was inaugurated, and the part which touched land on the Mercatello side had to be moved to an area that was more stable.

We now proceed to cross this narrow ribbon of cement suspended over the chasm. It can be crossed only on foot, though along the way one frequently comes across donkeys loaded with sacks and baskets. We are suspended over the void and on both sides are the deep valleys of the steep clay slopes, the *calanchi*, that have swallowed up the houses, the fields, the woods. The high sharp edges of the hard crests of clay protrude from the sandy hills.

If the wind is blowing when you cross over on the footbridge you almost feel dizzy or suffer from something like seasickness, for the valley of Civita is like a sea of sand, tossed by a thousand-year storm, with its high sharp waves and deep abysses which change profile and shape as they are constantly buffered by wind and rain; the pinnacles fall, the

Church of the Annunciation.
Left: **St. Joseph with Saint Rita of Cascia and St. Nicholas of Tolentino, painted on a wooden panel.**
Right: **Madonna and Child with Saints, by Giovan Francesco d'Avanzarano.**

precipices rise, and so it continues century after century.
Now we have finally reached Civita; the last steep climb crosses the place where another old neighborhood once stood, the quarter of the Ponte (the Bridge). It was an outpost located at the entrance to the city and was surrounded by great walls with watch towers and three gateways. Inside there was a church, a convent and a hospital. All of this is gone and only crumbling walls covered with weeds remain. Another neighborhood, the Contrada, has met a similar fate. To the left of the gate there are the ruins of the Palazzo Janni; here resided an ancient and illustrious family to which another saint from Bagnoregio belonged, Saint Bernard, who lived in the 8th century.

Passing through the Gate of Santa Maria we now enter the heart of the ancient acropolis, the *cassero* (from the Latin word *castrum* meaning a fortified place). This gate is the only way into the *castrum* and takes its name from a chapel dedicated to the Virgin which stood on the upper level and which has now disappeared as it was incorporated into the structure of a private home. The door is decorated with sculptures of two lions grasping human heads and are a reminder of the victorious battles waged by the people of Bagnoregio against the Monaldeschi family of Cervara and the Baglioni family of Torricella. At the top, in the center, there is the head of a lion rep-

Next page: **The end of the bridge of Civita with the ruins of the Janni Palazzo.**

resenting the symbol of the ancient Commune while the eagle is the emblem of the Cardinal-Governor Reginald Pole. In fact, it was Pole that commissioned the external decorations of the gate and Raffaele Sinibaldi from Montelupo who made them between 1554 and 1558. This gateway is regal yet simple and consists of an ogival arch surmounted by an elegant little loggia. As we proceed through the gate we can see that it is a 13th century structure which was built as a kind of superstructure over the original Etruscan-Roman façade which is deeply imbedded in the rock. The inside room with the two arches and the walls in *opus quadratum* (great squared off blocks of stone placed one on top of the other "a secco", i. e. with no mortar) are of certain Etruscan origin. Above, inside the gate there is a wooden beam with two large holes in which the wooden panels of the door turned, four great iron hinges and two guides for the portcullis: this is all that remains of the defense equipment of the city.

On the left there is a room which was once the headquarters for the guards, and is now used as a stall or tool shed.

If we now follow the Via Santa Maria we can observe the remains of a stone bench, which was also designed by Sinibaldi. This road leads to a little plaza on the right side of which we can observe the patrician residence of the Colesanti family, one of the most ancient and most important of the city. Other clean little houses face on to the square and next to them are narrow streets which run off into the void.

The street which we are following is an ancient *decumanus*, (the East-West axis of the Etruscan cities) which leads to the main plaza. Distances at Civita are never very great ! This square has always been the heart of the ancient village, where the *decumanus* intersects the *cardo* (the main street running from North to South). According to the complex Etruscan ritual which was followed for the foundation of a new city, once the site had

Next page: **Civita - the Gate of Santa Maria - the interior with the old opening partially excavated in the rock (called the Cave) which dates to the Etruscan era.**

The outside of the Gate of Santa Maria as it appeared after being remodeled in the 16th century by order of Cardinal Pole, whose emblem, the eagle, is placed above the arch.

been determined by the *aruspici* (soothsayers) on the basis of their interpretation of certain events, the perimeter of the city was marked out, and the main axis, consisting of a street running from East to West and one running from North to South. The point where they intersected was a sacred place, the *mundus*, a kind of sacrificial well which was connected by means of underground passageways to the necropolis which was built all around the city. On certain days offerings were made and funeral rites were held because on those days, through the *mundus*, it was possible for the living to communicate with the spirits of the dead.

Etruscan culture was profoundly imbued with religious feeling and a close bond existed between every day reality and the afterlife. For this reason the religious center of the city was also the place where the public buildings were located and where business was done according to a tradition which was later followed by the Romans with their forums. In our most ancient cities it is usual for the centers of religious and political activity of the Etruscan, Roman and Christian eras to all be found in the same place, built one on top of the other, with traditions and cultures superimposed, distant in time but not in space. The plaza where the old Cathedral, the City Hall and the palazzi of the nobles now stand was once surrounded by religious and civic buildings of the Etruscans and Romans. This is proved by the well (now covered over), the tunnels discovered years ago during construction work, and

Civita - Piazza San Donato, which has always been the center of activity for the town.

the fragments of archeological artifacts found scattered about almost everywhere in the surrounding buildings.

The façade that we see on the East side of the plaza is that of the church which was once the Cathedral of San Donato and has now been demoted to a simple parish church after the removal of the Bishopric to a safer site in Bagnoregio. On our right we can see the patrician palazzo of the Alemanni-Mazzocchi, which incorporates pre-existing structures and the ancient municipal bell-tower, into the present day building. A curious historical footnote: Annibale Caro, who translated the Aeneid into Italian, was a friend of the Alemanni family and often stayed here.

Next to it is the little palazzo of the Arcangeli, with a long bench of sculptured stone built into its base. This bench is actually the ogee molding from the Cathedral which was removed during restoration work and placed here in the 16th century.

Church of San Donato (in front of the church, remains of Roman columns are visible).

On the left, facing the former cathedral is the old Palazzo del Comune (City Hall) with the external stairway typical of the zone, the *profferlo*, (an element which is characteristic of civil architecture in the area around Viterbo and Orvieto), and the remains of a tower. The seat of the municipal government was moved here in 1448 after the original city hall located in the Mercatello neighborhood collapsed, and it was finally transferred to Bagnoregio in 1695.

At the base of the tower we can see the emblem of the Municipal slaughter-house and the *pietra del pesce* (the fish stone) which served as a fish shop. The slab of basalt on which the fish were displayed for sale is supported by a fragment of a Roman column.

Fragments of stone carvings of various eras (Roman and Early Medieval)) like these were used for the construction of the Cathedral and the bell-tower and are found throughout the buildings.

As we move toward San Donato we can observe that the church stands at the top of a brief stairway which is preceded by four granite columns, probably remnants of a pagan temple. Perhaps the original façade had a portico, as an ancient chronicle states. The present day building was remodeled many times; the Bishopric existed already in the year 600 AD

but the first certain date relative to the church is 1159, when a new main altar was built, as is mentioned in an inscription attached to the wall of the right nave. The floor plan is Romanesque, as demonstrated by the bell-tower, which has maintained its original appearance, but it was remodeled in 1511; the choir with the crypt below was torn down, the old presbytery was demolished, and a new one was built after the naves had been lengthened and the side walls raised. The façade was also redone in the style of the era, with new doors; the central door was made in 1524 by order of the Bishop Mercurio Vipera and the side ones in 1547, The tympanum was decorated with ceramic figures of Saint Donatus surrounded by angels (1593).

**San Donato:
the interior of the church.**

If one observes the bell-tower closely, it is possible to see the two basalt sarcophaguses which have been built into the walls along with their covers, and other artifacts on the side.

The vicissitudes of the church caused by remodeling, earthquake damage, and restoration work which is still going on, can best be seen inside; some of the Romanesque windows were walled up so that Baroque altars could be placed over them (some of them have been removed), the columns, which probably were removed from pagan buildings, were covered up and transformed into pilasters (only a few of them now have their original appearance after partial restoration), and the decorations were covered with plaster, some of which has now been removed. The stairway which leads to the presbytery is obviously built with material taken from older buildings, archeological artifacts, basket-weave carved bas-reliefs, and Lombard motifs. Material of this type is scattered throughout the church: fragments of consoles, slabs and stones; the recycling of decorative stone work from pagan buildings for use in Christian churches was a normal procedure in this era.

At the entrance to the church, on the right, we can observe a little urn with the image of Saint Victoria on the inside. This saint was martyred in 251 AD under the emperor Decius in the

Church of San Donato.
From left to right: **the 19th century reliquary
of St. Hildebrand, a native of
Bagnoregio who lived
in the 9th century;
the urn containing the remains
of St. Victoria, one of the two
Patron Saints of the city.**

town of Trebula Metuesca, now called Monteleone Sabina. Her remains were brought here during the barbarian invasions because Civita was thought to be a safer place, and were preserved in this improvised urn made out of a hollowed out fragment of Roman entablature until 1782, when they were finally placed in a new urn under the altar of St. Peter in the chapel to the left of the main altar. Noteworthy, also, is the second painting, in the right nave, made in 1606 by an anonymous artist; depicting the birth of the Virgin, and Saints Francis, Bonaventure, and Victoria with Civita and Mercatello in the background. The painting is a precious document which tells us how the city looked in the 17th century.

In the next altar panel, painted in the late 16th century, we

The Madonna of the Rosary with Saints Dominic and Catherine, by Giuseppe Fretti (1824).

again find St. Bonaventure and St. Victoria at the feet of the Virgin, with St. Thomas and St. Donatus who is holding a little model of the church which is dedicated to him. Halfway down the nave hangs a processional banner made in 1674 by the Viterbese painter Francesco Ciacci. It is painted on both sides, as was the custom, and in its rather naif style depicts the population of Civita invoking the Madonna on the front, and, on the back, Saint Bonaventure protecting his city, and, again, in this case, images of places that have disappeared long ago.

Over the altar at the far end of the church, we can admire the stupendous Crucifix, the most interesting piece of art work in the church. This is a 15th century wooden sculpture which recalls the style of Donatello. According to tradition, in 1499, during a terrible plague, a devout woman who had already been stricken with the disease was praying before the holy image when she suddenly heard it say distinctly: "With thee, woman, the plague will end". And, in fact, she was the last victim, because the plague ended immediately afterward. If one observes the Crucifix from different directions it almost seems to change expression: dying from the left, still alive seen from the front, dead seen from the right. The statue is deeply moving for its realism and the intensity of the expression. The arms are moveable and the crucifix is removed from the cross and laid on a litter for the traditional procession on Good Friday. Every year on that day, at 9 o'clock in the evening, the participants in the procession, dressed in costumes and carrying torches, accompany the miraculous image of Christ from the old Cathedral to Bagnoregio, and the drama of the Passion is re-enacted amidst the crowds. But before midnight it is quickly returned to its own church because traditions states that, if it is left in Bagnoregio, Civita will disappear forever from the face of the earth.

The niche in which the Crucifix is kept was created in 1855 by tearing out the apse with the 16th century frescoes which had been commissioned by the Bishop, Ferdinand of Castile, who had had the church enlarged. Only the fragments with the figures of St. Bonaventure and St. Jerome were saved.

Under the altar there is an urn containing the ashes of Hildebrand, another famous saint from this city. He was Bishop of Bagnoregio from 856 to 873 and was such a consistent example of virtue and humility that even during his lifetime it was said that he was able to work miracles. For this reason immediately after his death he was proclaimed a Saint by popular

Church of San Donato. "Madonna Liberatrice", fragment of a fresco attributed to the Umbrian school, which suddenly reappeared when the plaster covering it fell off during the earthquake of 1695.
Below, left to right: The Baptismal Font made of stone elements of various eras; on the left of the photograph is the cabinet for the holy oil with carvings of the della Robbia school; Holy water stoop made out of two ancient capitals.

San Donato - the movingly realistic 15th century Crucifix.

Detail of the head of the Christ.

demand and made Patron Saint of the city along with the pre-existing patroness and protectress, St. Victoria. The people of Bagnoregio are very zealous in honoring him because this Saint has a reputation of being very severe with those who do not treat him with all due respect. The reliquary was made in 1862 by the Roman sculptor Stefano Scevola.

The main altar is 18th century and includes beautiful wooden sculptures by M. Calcioni, an artist from Foligno. Another important work in the church are the choir stalls made in 1630 by the Flemish artist Alberto Joris.

On the left is the altar dedicated to St. Peter. Only a few fragments of the original 16th century decorations still remain in the apse, but it is possible to see a fragment of the Deposition which was discovered and restored in 1971. Below there is a glass urn which contains the remains of St. Victoria, enclosed in a sculpture by G. F. Vitené (1886).

In the left nave there is a fresco depicting the *Birth of St. John the Baptist* by the famous Orvietan artist, Cesare Nebbia. In the foreground we can see the women busy taking care of the newborn baby, and in the background, the Virgin Mary and St. Elizabeth (1556).

Immediately next to it is the altar of the *Madonna Liberatrice* to which the people of Civita are particularly devoted. This Renaissance fresco, in which it is possible to discern the influence of Perugino, came to light when the plaster which covered it over fell off during the earthquake of 1695. In fact, in times of plague it had been common use to cover walls of public buildings with lime plaster in order to disinfect them, so that it is not surprising that the fresco had been white-washed. Its appearance under such exceptional circumstances was considered almost miraculous, and ever since then the prodigious event has been celebrated annually on the first Sunday of June, with various festivities and contests, the most characteristic of which is the *Tonna*, a donkey race on an improvised track set up in the plaza in front of the church.

Noteworthy, also, is the stone Baptismal Font, made up of parts from earlier

From left to right: **San Donato - the processional banner made by Francesco Ciacci for a local Confraternity, the Company of St. Peter, which shows the Virgin surrounded by Her Faithful; the back of the same banner, with St. Bonaventure protecting the city of Civita. The painting presents a rare image of the way Civita looked before the earthquake of 1695.**

Below, left to right: **Civita - the entrance to the Bishop's Palace; remains of the Bishopric.**

**Fresco of the Umbrian School
with the Madonna and Child
with Saints Sebastian
and Pantaleon.
The painting is kept inside
the old Bishopric which
is now a private home.**

works, and the tabernacle for holding the holy oil, which was originally used to keep the Eucharist, according to the inscription on the stone: *Ecce panis angelorum.* On the stone, traces of polychrome decorations, in a Renaissance style that recalls Luca della Robbia, are still visible.

As we leave the church, on our right we can see the little square with the ancient Bishopric and the bell-tower on one side and, on the other, the *Palazzo di Giustizia* or Tribunal with the windows of the prison section covered with bars, and what remains of the Bishop's Palace, most of which collapsed during the earthquake of 1695. This has been transformed into a house and inside it there is still a fresco of the School of Perugino with the *Madonna and Child with Saints Sebastian and Pantaleon* with a soft Umbrian landscape in the background.. The figure of the Bishop Ferdinand of Castile, who commissioned the painting, is visible on the left. Ferdinand was appointed governor of Bagnoregio by Pope Alexander VI Borgia, a fellow Spaniard, in May of 1500 and had many improvements made in the church, the Bishop's Palace and the garden. Very little remains of the lovely garden which was done in true Italian style with its flower-beds surrounded by boxwood hedges and decorated with archeological artifacts like columns, capitals and sarcophaguses. Even the house where St. Bonaventure was born has collapsed and the only reminder of its existence is the little tabernacle recently built there, which can be reached by following the narrow pathway behind the Mazzocchi-Alemanni Palazzo on the right of the square. This pathway comes to an abrupt end at the precipice and if we look over the edge it is possible to see fragments of the walls that are all that remains of the Fidanza house. Devout citizens had transformed the house into a church which was severely damaged by the 1695 earthquake, after which it was rebuilt and then collapsed entirely in a landslide in the 19th century. The portion of walls that it was possible to recover were reused in1846 to build a chapel dedicated to the Saint inside the church of St. Francis. This latter was built in the new part of the city and took the name of another place that is connected to the life of St. Bonaventure, the convent where he took holy orders, which fell down in 1746 after yet another landslide caused by an earthquake.

If we now continue our walk along the right side of the

church we will be in a street called Via Maestà because it led to another church where an Enthroned Madonna (Maestà) was venerated.

Against the walls of the ex-Cathedral we can see various ancient artifacts: parts of sarcophaguses and entablatures and stones carved with the basket-weave motif which is typical of the Early Middle Ages. To the right and left, the cross streets come to an abrupt end at the brink of the chasm, so we must proceed on the central road which descends toward the Valley of the Tiber.

This was where the East gate to the city once stood; it was called the gate "of the Maestà" after the church of the same name. Both have disappeared and so has the entire neighborhood called the Carcere which once stood to our right. From this point there is a view across the desolate valley which was once covered with fields and forests. Now the narrow valleys are separated by sharp pinnacles with picturesque names like Montione, the Cathedral, Chiccoro Rosso, Pianale, Ponticelli. The road continues on across a ledge cut into the tufa stone and passes in front of some caves (the old dove-cotes) and finally reaches a tunnel dug in the rock, which is called the Bucaione and crosses all of Civita from North to South. This is an ancient *dromos*, which was the access corridor leading to an Etruscan necropolis; it was later used as a conduit for drinking water. In 1931 after the collapse of one of the mule paths that was used by the farmers of Civita to reach the fields to the

Next page: **The ancient Etruscan dromos (corridor) which is now used as an access road to the valley of the calanchi. It is called the "Bucaione" (the big hole) and crosses the entire town from North to South.**

east of the town, it was decided to widen the *dromos* so that it could be used as a footpath. Though it is now little used by the farmers, it is convenient for reaching the beautiful chestnut woods or for adventuring out on to the sand hills.

If we turn back to gaze at the city we see what Bonaventure Tecchi described: *"all that remains - a little huddle of ruined houses and walls, a dark shape on the rock, perched above the void – seems to breathe its last breath."*

From one year to the next, imperceptibly but inexorably, the landscape of Civita changes: a fragment of wall falls down, a part of the road or the parapet disappears in a landslide. By observing old photographs it is possible to see just how much of the town has been erased by time. This feeling of imminent catastrophe, a catastrophe which is somehow always being put off, is very moving and gives Civita an atmosphere of sweet sadness.

But the people of Civita, so desperately attached to their little fragment of rock, are not resigned to the idea of living in a Museum-city or in a ghost town. They are determined to keep alive and intact this fragile, precious reminder of the past and to imagine a life for Civita in the future, a rare example of courage and a challenge beyond hope.

View from the bell-tower of the old city hall (Palazzo Comunale) which incorporates a tower which has had the top portion knocked off; on the left is the Mazzocchi-Alemanni Palace.

LA TONNA

The Tonna *is a typical celebration that takes place once a year in Civita: it is a donkey race around a circular track set up in the main square.*

Considering the unusual conditions in which the people of Civita live, the donkey has become an almost indispensable means of transportation, and is ideal for riding up to the fields nestled among the cliffs and for going back and forth between Civita and Bagnoregio. In fact, there are no roads, but only steep pathways across the sand hills, and automobiles are not allowed on the narrow bridge connecting the two towns.

For this reason these animals, which have almost disappeared from the scene in other parts of Italy, are very common in Civita where they can be seen walking patiently with heavy loads of firewood, and sacks and baskets full of goods. This is the reason why the people of Civita are particularly attached to their donkeys, and have, in fact founded an association with the purpose of studying ways to improve the particular breed of donkeys and promote their use, also in other towns.

Why and when this ancient donkey race began are not known, but on the occasion of the Tonna the normally

sleepy little town of Civita becomes suffused with excitement and heated rivalries are created similar to those which occur in Siena for the famous Palio horse race.

Twice a year, on the first Sunday in June and again in mid-September, in preparation for the race which is held in the main plaza of Civita, which has been left unpaved specifically for this purpose, poles are inserted into the earth at a distance of about 2 yards each from the other and connected by a rope in order to lay out the race course. The circular track takes up almost the whole plaza and is just wide enough for two donkeys to run one next to the other.

The donkey race begins in the afternoon after a brief procession.

Usually about twelve donkeys participate, with volunteer jockeys and they represent the various neighborhoods or contrada of Civita. They start two at a time and have to run around the track three times. One of the donkeys is eliminated each time until the winner is declared and the contrada it represents will win the much desired palio.

The donkey in pagan antiquity was considered a noble, intelligent animal, and only in a later era came to be a symbol of laziness and ignorance; during the tonna he regains his former stature as a protagonist.

The plaza decorated with colored banners becomes an amphitheater with people crowded at the windows, on the porches and balconies, the stairways or wherever there is space and the air is filled with whistles and cheers of every kind in the colorful local dialect.

The Tonna is an authentic people's festivity which the people of Civita experience with conviction and passion.

ESSENTIAL BIBLIOGRAPHY

Tuscia Viterbese – Rome, 1968.

L'ambiente, la memoria, il progetto - Testimonianze su Civita di Bagnoregio. Milano, 1988.

B. BARBINI – *Il Risorgimento della Tuscia.* Viterbo, 1983.

P. BORMIOLI, M. CAGIANO DE AZEVEDO – *Civita di Bagnoregio,* Roma 1982.

F. MACCHIONI – *Storia di Bagnoregio dai tempi antichi al 1503.* Viterbo, 1955.

G. MEDORI – *Civita di Bagnoregio - Guida turistica,* 1982.

F. PIETRANGELI PAPINI – *La Battaglia di Bagnorea.* Roma, 1965.

F. PIETRANGELI PAPINI – *Bagnoregio - Cronologia storica.* Viterbo, 1972.

E. RAMACCI – *Ultimo statuto della città di Bagnoregio,* 1984.

E. RAMACCI – *Bagnoregio e Civita.* Montefiascone, 1986.

M. SIGNORELLI – *Civita di Bagnoregio nella storia.* Viterbo, 1979.

B. TECCHI – *La vedova timida (racconti).* Milano, 1942.